Making Photography Easy

Book 2
in
Quick Tips from a
Pro Photographer
Series

by Julia Harwood

Table of Contents

1. Introduction

For those of you who enjoyed my first mini book, welcome back, to those of you who are new you can get book 1 here:as an ebook
http://www.amazon.com/dp/B00T81L52E
or here as a printed book here
https://www.createspace.com/5454887?ref=1147694&utm_id=6026

2. What settings do I start with?

People often get stuck on, "where do I start?" So here are some minimum settings to help you.

First step is to use the scene modes that come with the camera, sometimes they are SP or they may be icons of mountains, a person, someone running etc. These have the settings optimized for that situation.

So if you want to learn manual, take a photo on scene mode, then look at the settings and manually set the camera to the same settings and then work from there.

Now if you want more control or the scene mode isn't working then start here:

Minimum settings

These will help you get that shot without blur from camera shake.

Hand holding a camera we want the shutter speed to be at least 1/60 sec shutter speed.
This works up to a focal length of 60mm, after that we have a formula to use, yes this is the tricky part but stay with me and I will explain, so we also need the shutter speed to be at least the inverse of the focal length, this means, if you have a focal length of 80mm then your shutter speed needs to be at least 1/80 sec. If your focal length is 100mm then your shutter speed will need to be 1/100, if your focal length is 250mm then your shutter speed will need to be 1/250, see it's very easy!!

80mm = 1/80 shutter speed
100mm = 1/100 shutter speed
250mm = 1/250 shutter speed.

Do you see the pattern?

Now on top of this we have minimum shutter speed for certain situations, these all assume you are using a focal length of up to 60mm. Over this you will need to add on the focal length.

So to recap,
- 1/60 minimum to hand hold your camera.

 - Formula for over 60mm focal length as
    explained above.

For specific situations, shutter speeds will need to be higher, so these are listed below.

(Remember if using more than 60mm focal length then add the inverse of the focal length as well)

2.1. People

- **People**

- standing still, posing 1/60.

- walking 1/80

- jogging 1/120

- running, swimming 1/160

- Children 1/120 (*this is because children are rarely still*:))

This is the same even on a tripod, because these settings are what is needed to stop the motion of the person breathing, blinking, walking, running etc.

- An aperture of between f2.5 and f5.6 is best for portraits or f5.6 to f8 for group images. This focuses on the person/people while blurring the background

 - Always use a focal length between 50mm and 105mm for people and animals as this is the most flattering. (Unless you want to make someone look like a clown:)

A note here on tripods. If you have image stabilization on your camera or lens you need to turn it off when using a tripod or the camera will introduce motion of its own. Some of the latest cameras have a tripod mode under image stabilization so you can use this.

Put a sticker on the top of the tripod saying is IS off? This will remind you and when you take the camera off the tripod it will act as a memory jogger to help remind you to turn it back on.

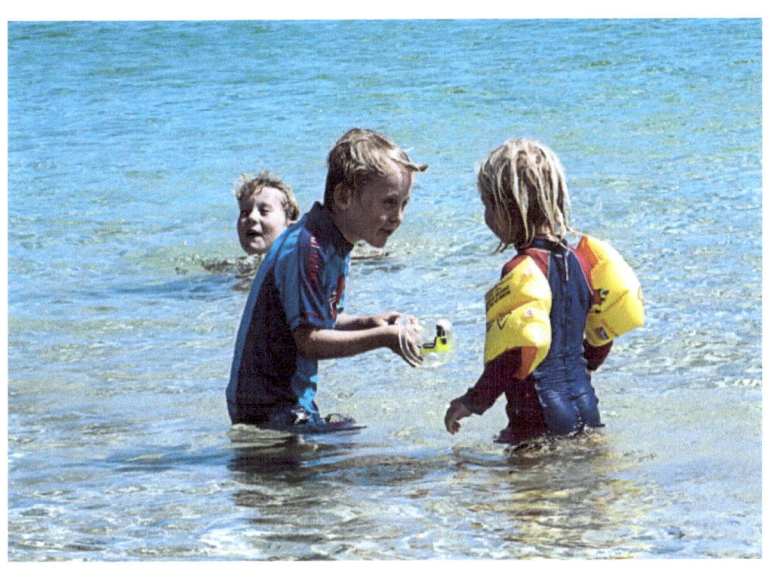

2.2. Animals

Animals
- sitting or lying down sleeping 1/60
- walking 1/120
- running 1/200

I generally use an aperture of f5.6 to f8 as this helps you to make sure the animal is captured in focus, or if you want the whole scene in focus f11 or higher. If the animal is sleeping or in a zoo and you want to blur the surroundings, then use f2.8 and focus on the animals eyes.

NB -
For animals, birds, children, or sports shoot in <u>burst</u> <u>mode</u> so you don't miss that special moment.

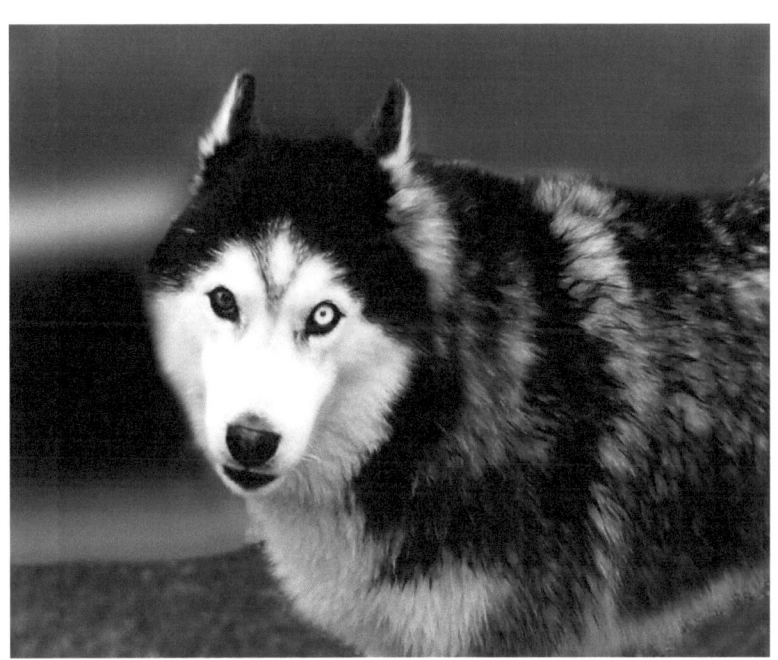

2.3. Birds

Birds

- 1/80 if still,

- if flying depends on bird,

- large slower birds 1/500,

- small quick birds like finches or honey-eaters 1/750, but the faster the better.

Again I usually go with as wide an aperture as I can, while still getting a good shutter speed. I recommend starting at f5.6

NB -
For animals, birds, children, or sports shoot in <u>burst</u> <u>mode</u> so you don't miss that special moment.

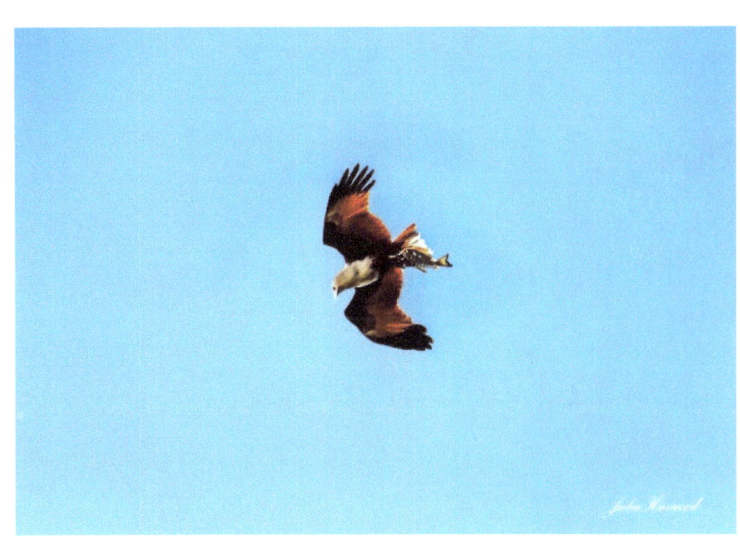

2.4. Cars

Cars

- driving normally 1/200

- racing 1/500 or more.

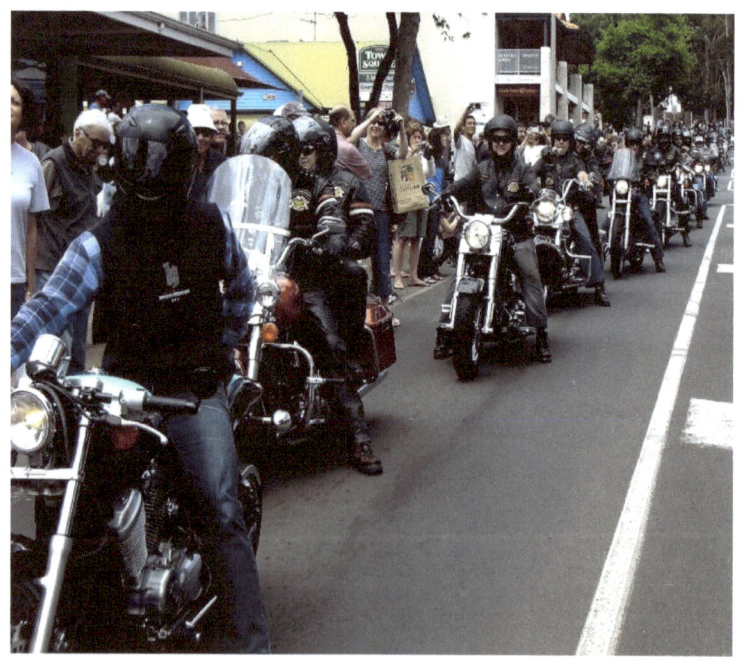

2.5. Landscapes

- **hand held** is a minimum shutter speed1/60,

- aperture is best as large as possible, f11 to f32, this gives us a large depth of field, which just means more of the image is in focus.

- generally a wide focal length, 24mm up. *(If we go too wide we will get lens distortion and need to adjust in   post possessing.)*

- On a **tripod,** as slow as you want as long as there are no moving objects. Aperture stays the same as above.

Remember trees and flowers move in the wind so on a still day you are fine, on a windy day you will have to increase your shutter speed. Usually around dawn is the calmest time.

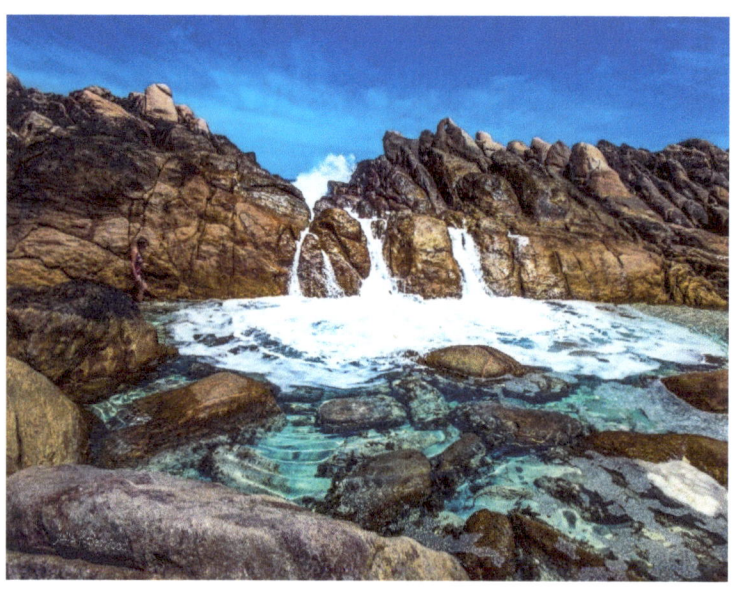

To freeze motion

- Light breeze 1/80,

- breezy 1/160.

You can use a slower shutter speed if you want to add motion blur to the image.

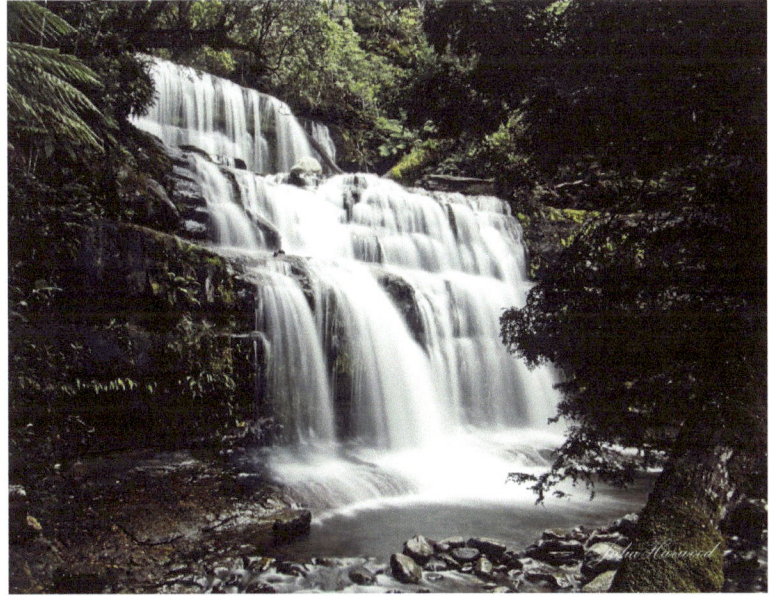

2.6. Light Trails

Light trails

You will need a <u>tripod</u> or a way to stabilize your camera and a <u>remote shutter release</u> or use the <u>timer function</u> on your camera to eliminate shutter shake.

Also if your camera has a mirror and you are using long shutter speeds you will need to go to <u>live view</u> to lock the mirror so that you don't get movement from mirror slap, also remember to turn <u>image stabilization off</u>.

Start at 1/2 second.
Aperture of f8 upwards.
Then adjust your shutter speed up or down to get the effect you want.

Down to 1 sec or longer for longer trails and back up to ¼ or 1/8 for shorter trails or brighter areas.

2.7. Fireworks

You will need a <u>tripod</u> or a way to stabilize your camera and a <u>remote shutter release</u> or use the <u>timer function</u> on your camera to eliminate shutter shake.

2 to 3 secs, this allows you to get multiple bursts in the frame.

Remember to turn your camera to portrait orientation and use a remote shutter release or your timer function.

You can use a focal length of anywhere from f5.6 to f8

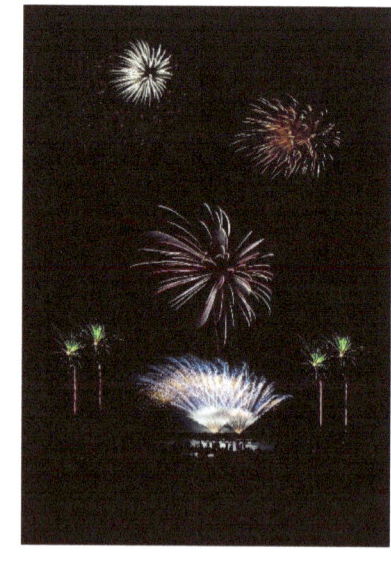

Star trails

You will need a <u>tripod</u> or a way to stabilize your camera and a <u>remote shutter release</u> or use the <u>timer function</u> on your camera to eliminate shutter shake.

- minimum 30sec up to as long as you like but be careful of battery running too low.

- f8 and focus on infinity. (You may need to go to manual focus, set it as far as it will go and then bring it back a little.)

- ISO3200 (start at this for 30 sec and see how it goes, you may be able to bring it down to around ISO800, so experiment and see.)

- wide focal length

At 30 seconds you will have to take a series of images and join them in post processing, to capture in camera use 1 hour or more.

To do this you use bulb mode, usually marked B on the top dial and you need a remote that locks so that it will stay open until you release it, otherwise you have to sit there the whole time with your finger holding the shutter button down!

There are other requirements for this that I will cover in the night photography book.

2.8. Water

- to freeze water 1/60 to 1/500 depending on how fast water is moving.

 - For silky water 3 sec for a slow stream and up to 30 sec for a fast flowing waterfall.

If only want water in focus try f4.5 or if you want everything in focus, f11 or higher.

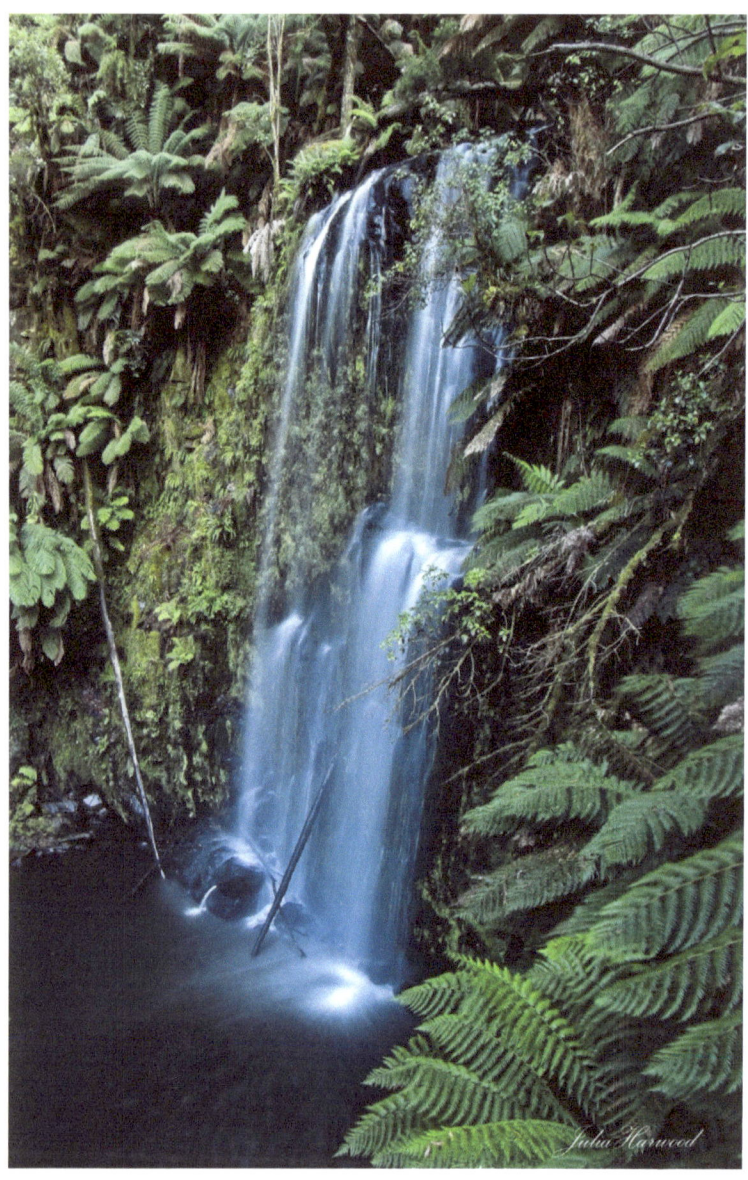

Julia Harwood

2.9. Flowers

-1/60 if still

- 1/100 if slight breeze, but usually you won't want to be shooting flowers in a breeze as it is too hard to focus correctly.

Set camera to macro

Try to eliminate any wind or shoot early in the morning when the air is usually calmer.

- Use a maximum depth of field, at least f11 (this is because in macro our focal plane becomes a lot narrower)

If you want to freeze any movement use some fill flash.

Fill flash is where your flash is set to lower than full power. You can usually set this in your camera menu.

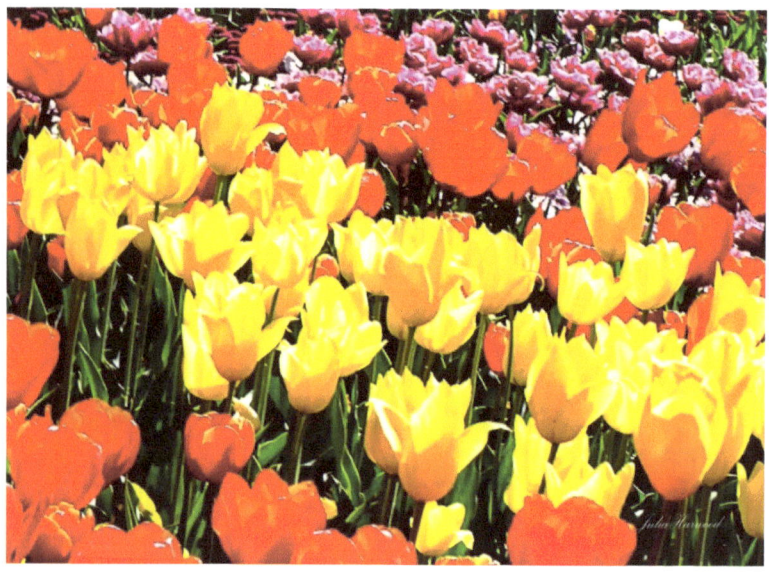

2.10. Extra tips

These are starting guidelines, you have to work to the conditions you have, but it helps to know roughly where to start so that you can just adjust from here. There is a lot of debate about what the formula should be for hand holding a camera and other situations, but this book is about making photography easy, so we are not going to get bogged down with the debate here, instead I will add that these settings work most of the time, some people have steadier hands than others so the settings will vary, also the more you want to enlarge the image the faster your shutter speed should be to get the sharpest image.

But these are some settings to get you started.

If you find your images are a bit shaky then increase the settings to accommodate.

Always stop for a moment and check in your LCD screen, zooming in to check for movement. Missing one or two shots early will be made up for by having many other great shots rather than coming home excited only to find all the images are blurred.

3. Gear

Another question I am often asked is what do I need to take with me?

So here is a general idea.

Minimum equipment

- Camera body, point and shoot or bridge camera

 - lens, a good zoom is a great all purpose lens

 OR

- For landscapes generally a wide angle lens

- for portraits a 50-105mm or a prime lens in this range.

- birds or sports a telephoto (long) lens.

- batteries

- memory card
 - phone with a camera.

Sometimes we get hung up on gear when in actual fact all we need to get started is the basics.

I also recommend (depending on what you are shooting)
- a tripod and remote shutter release,

- a UV filter to protect your lens, it is a lot cheaper to replace a scratched UV filter than the whole lens.

- After that a polarising filter

- a graduated ND filter

- a set of reflectors

- an external flash.

A lot of the gear you need will depend on what you like shooting so I will cover it in the e-book for that topic.

If you are shooting a wedding or important event you will want a spare camera body and a second lens.

A lot of wedding photographers have the main camera set up with their prime 50mm lens and then a spare body with a zoom that also covers the 50-110mm range. This gives them more options when shooting and also means if a camera or lens stops working they still have an alternative......and believe me it does happen!

I carry my main camera and a point and shoot that can shoot RAW images as well as my iPhone of course.

Most cameras come with either one or two lenses.

For portraiture you want to be shooting between 50-110mm, I like the effect of 75mm.

Depending on what you like shooting most you may want a wide angle, I have a 24mm for landscapes, if you like sports and action you are going to want as long a focal length as you can afford and preferably a zoom so that you can capture the action without having to move much.

If you want to do macro there are specialist macro lenses or you can use extension tubes, we will cover this more in the macro book.

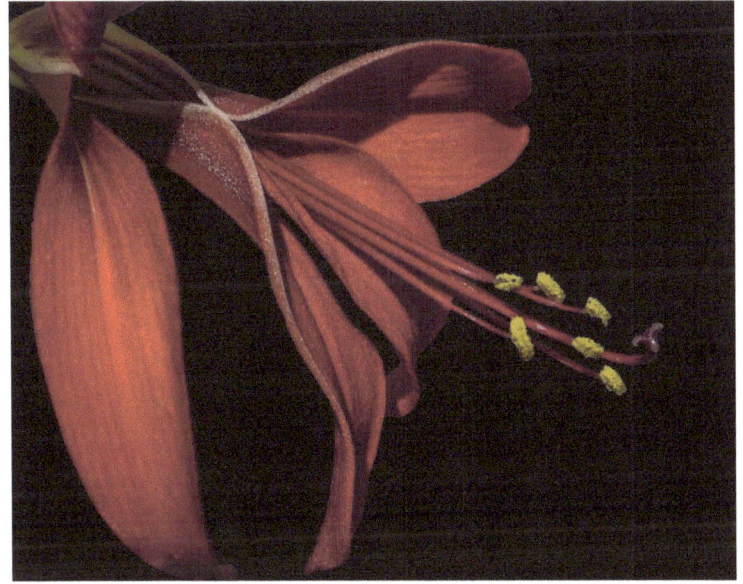

4. Packing a photo bag

What to have in it and what precautions to take.

- A padded camera bag, you are carrying expensive gear, so you want to protect it from falls. Make sure you also have a rain cover for the camera bag and a plastic cover for the camera, a shower cap works well for the camera. Place shower cap around body of camera with opening at the lens end, then place an elastic band around the open part of the shower cap and the lens to hold the cap tight so that water doesn't run down the length of the lens and into the working parts of the lens or camera.

- If you are shooting in very hot or very cold weather get a thermal bag, like the freezer ones from the supermarket and keep your gear in that. Batteries go flat quickly when cold so a good idea is to keep them in an inside pocket of your jacket where your body heat will keep them warm and in the heat your camera can get too warm which can cause issues with the image, especially by creating extra noise and jpeg artifacts.

Make sure you have space for

- your camera

- lenses

- cleaning cloths

- spare batteries

- memory cards (try to have two spots, one for cards ready to be used and one for full cards.)

- chargers

- filters

I also carry a small first aid kit, waterproof matches, a pen and paper, water and some snacks.

A bag that allows you to attach your tripod is handy too.

Remember safety first, let someone know where you are going and an expected return time.

If it is a dangerous area take someone with you.

This also applies if you are trying for that exclusive shot, don't put yourself in harms way, if you are going out on a ledge, check it first and stay well back from the edge.

Always obey safety signs and remember also, that your family consider you are far more important than that shot.

5. Setting white balance

This can be one of the easiest things or it can be something that ruins a lot of images so it's worth taking the time to get it right.

If you shoot in RAW you can set the white balance when you process the image but as many people shoot both RAW and JPEG it still pays to get it right in camera.

The easiest and most traditional way is to carry a grey card.

You can get them cheap online, or there are tutorials available on how to make your own.

I have managed to get a lens cover that doubles as a grey card which is great as I always have it with me and if I accidentally leave the lens cap on I just tell them that I was setting the white balance :)

To use the grey card you place it in the scene you are shooting and take a shot, there is usually a menu shortcut for you to use in order to set the white balance but if not you can set the white balance from the grey card in the image when you process the shot.

Most cameras have a range of white balance (WB) options. The best way to see how they work is to take a series of images of the same thing at the same time going through each of the white balance settings and then comparing them when you upload the photos. You can get some really great effects this way as well.

Sunny white balance is for days when there are no clouds around and it gives you a really cool image, if you want a warmer image, even on a sunny day you can use the Shade white balance or the cloudy white balance as well as using them on the cloudy days.

There are also settings for tungsten and fluorescent lighting, which are the two most common types of indoor lighting. So use these settings when shooting indoors as this will prevent you getting a color cast from these lights.

6. Time of day

I spoke about 'cool' and 'warm' images, these are terms we use to describe the light

- Cool is more the blue tones you get in shadows and in the middle of the day

- Warm light is the golden light we get at the beginning and end of the day, which is why sunset and sunrise are often referred to as the "golden hours".

There is also a time after the sun has set and before it goes full Black, this is known as the blue hour.

We also group lighting into hard and soft lighting.

- Hard light is when we have strong shadows and highlights. This is great for sculpting an image or depicting the hardness of a person or object. For example if you were shooting a boxer or a prison guard you may want to use hard lighting.

- Soft light is when the transition from highlights to shadows is very subtle and looks much more natural and flattering. We usually try to use this for women and children. It is also great for landscapes as it allows us to see much more detail in the shadow areas.

The best photos for portraits and landscapes are usually shot during the golden hours because the light is soft and the shadows aren't harsh and they are warm and we are drawn to warm images.

However if you are trying to depict a scene of devastation you want the cold harsh light to emphasize the feeling you are trying to portray.

Clouds are often referred to as "natures softbox" as they diffuse the light and make it soft, this works great for portraits and for flowers or macro images as it gives nice even light. Soft light is where we have a large light source *(in relation to the subject)*.

The harsh sun in the middle of the day is when we have a very direct small light source *(in relation to the subject)*.

As we go through the subjects in the mini books I will tell you what is best for that subject and what to do if you have to shoot under adverse conditions.

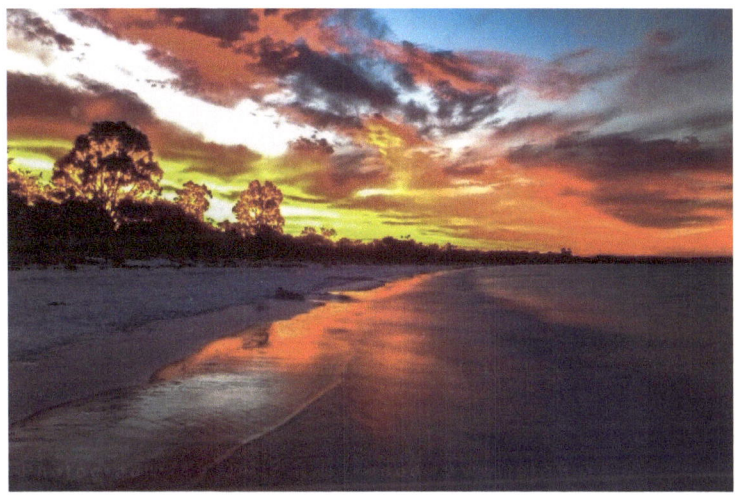

7. Staying motivated

This is often the hardest thing for photographers. One way that I have found works is to set yourself weekly goals, another is to start a project, a great one is 52 images in a year, so that's one a week, set up a Pinterest account and make a board for your images and upload one each week, you can extend this to 2 x 52 or you can do 365 days.

Pick a theme, it can be as broad as, 'things we are thankful for' or as narrow as a single color, or better yet create a rainbow.

Another way is to join a photographic community, local or online, there are lots on sites such as Google Plus (G+), Flickr, Ipernity, etc. Spend time looking at others photos, asking questions and learning.

Another way is to take a structured course, one I recommend is called "the Dash" and can help you work at whatever level you are at. To find out more go to **http://www.digital-photo-secrets.com/aff/Jkh/20854b63.html**

There are also lots of free tutorials online, so be sure to search for them and of course I have some tutorials and lots of links on my website at http://www.juliaharwood.com

8. Cheat Sheet

Making photography easier - Min Settings
People - standing still, posing 1/60.
- walking 1/80
- jogging 1/120
- running, swimming 1/160
- Children 1/120
- *appature* between f2.5 and f5.6 is best for portraits   or f5.6 to f8 for groups
- *focal length* 50mm - 105mm

Tripod
− IS off, and use timer or remote.

Hand holding 1/60 sec or the inverse of the focal length
100mm = 1/100
200mm = 1/200

Animals - sitting or lying down sleeping 1/60
Fireworks 2 to 3 secs, Camera to portrait orientation

Min Equipment
- Camera body, point and shoot or bridge camera
 - lens
 - batteries

- memory card
- phone with a camera.
- a tripod and remote shutter release,
- a UV filter, polarising filter, graduated ND filter
- a set of reflectors
- an external flash.
- small first aid kit, waterproof matches, a pen and paper, water and some snacks.
- use a remote shutter release or your timer function.
- focal length of anywhere from F5.6 on.

Star trails
- minimum 30sec max depend on battery life
- f8 and focus on infinity.
- ISO3200 - ISO800
- wide focal length

Water - to freeze water 1/60 to 1/500
- For silky water 3 sec up to 30 sec

Flowers -1/60 if still 1/100 if slight breeze, macro. maximum depth of field, at least f11
Freeze movement - fill flash.
            - walking 1/120
            - running 1/200

Birds - 1/80 if still,
            - if flying depends on bird,
            - large slower birds 1/500,
            - small quick birds like finches or
              honey-eaters 1/750

Burst mode – animals, children, sports

Cars - driving normally 1/200
- racing 1/500

Light Trails Start at 1/2 second. Aperture of f8 up.

Landscapes
- **hand held** is a minimum shutter speed1/60, tripod – any.
- aperture is best as large as possible, f11 to f32
- generally a wide focal length, 24mm up.

To freeze motion - Light breeze 1/80, breezy 1/160.